Maggots, Grubs, and More

The SECRET Lives of Young Insects

Melissa Stewart

The Millbrook Press   Brookfield, Connecticut

For Charlie, Allison,
Jacob, and Justin

Cover photograph courtesy of
Animals Animals (© Patti Murray)

Photographs courtesy of Bruce Coleman, Inc.: pp. 4
(© Fritz Polking), 20 (© Laura Riley), 43 (© Robert
P. Carr), 54 (© Jeff Foott); Peter Arnold, Inc.: pp.
10 (© M. & C. Photography), 11 (© Keith Kent),
40 (© Hans Pfletschinger); Photo Researchers, Inc.:
pp. 13 (© Larry Cameron), 15 (© William M.
Partington), 19 (© M. H. Sharp), 22 (© David T.
Roberts/Nature's Images, Inc.), 32 (© J. H.
Robinson), 37 (© David M. Schleser), 42 (© John
Mitchell), 50 (© Kenneth H. Thomas), 51 (©
Stephen P. Parker); © Michael Burnett: p. 16;
Animals Animals: pp. 24 (© Raymond A. Mendez),
31 (© Breck P. Kent), 39 (© Anthony Bannister),
53 (© Patti Murray), 55 (© Patti Murray), 56
(© Patti Murray); Visuals Unlimited, Inc.: pp. 25
(© Don Fawcett), 27 (© Rob Simpson), 28
(© David Wrobel), 45 (© Wally Eberhart), 47
(© E. S. Ross), 52 (© Bill Beatty); © Andrew
A. Skolnick: pp. 29, 49

Library of Congress Cataloging-in-Publication Data

Stewart, Melissa.
Maggots, grubs, and more: the secret
lives of young insects/Melissa Stewart.
p. cm.
Summary: Describes the life cycles
of a variety of insects.
Includes bibliographical references (p.   ).
ISBN 0-7613-2658-8 (lib. bdg.)
1. Insects—Infancy—Juvenile literature.
2. Insects—Juvenile literature.
[1. Insects.]   I. Title.
QL495.5.S74   2003
595.713'9—dc21   2002013965

Published by The Millbrook Press, Inc.
2 Old New Milford Road
Brookfield, Connecticut 06804
www.millbrookpress.com

Contents

Introduction
Two Kinds of Young Insects

Imagine a pesky mosquito buzzing around your head. Think of a giant dragonfly hovering above a pond. Picture a busy bumblebee collecting pollen from a brightly colored flower. You've seen all these adult insects many times. But do you know what they looked like while they were growing up?

Adult mosquitoes and dragonflies spend a lot of time flying through the air, but when they are young they spend all their time underwater. Adult bees and ants are easy to spot as they rest on flowers or scurry across the ground, but as youngsters they never leave their nests. Young grasshoppers live out in the open, but they look so similar to their parents that you might not even notice the difference.

Just like humans, insects go through many changes as they grow. When you were a newborn baby, you looked different, and acted differently than you do now. When you are a teenager, you will go through many more changes. Humans grow and change a little bit at a time, but insects go through a series of distinct growth stages called **metamorphosis**.

We've all seen adult dragonflies, but have you ever seen them when they are young? Some young insects look very similar to adults, while others look different.

Some insects go through simple metamorphosis, which includes three separate growth stages. Grasshoppers, cockroaches, giant water bugs, and dragonflies begin as eggs, hatch to become **nymphs**, and then transform into adults. Other insects go through a more complex, four-step growth process called complete metamorphosis. Houseflies, mosquitoes, ladybugs, ants, and butterflies begin as eggs, hatch to become **larvae**, change into **pupae**, and finally transform into adults.

All young insects are very hungry when they hatch. Because larvae and nymphs spend most of their time feeding, their bodies are perfectly designed for finding, eating, and digesting food.

The more food a young insect eats, the faster it grows. Eventually, the insect's insides press against its hard outer coat. This **exoskeleton** is like a suit of armor. It keeps an insect's body moist and helps protect it from enemies.

When an insect outgrows its exoskeleton, it stops eating and remains quiet and still. Within a few hours, the hard case splits down the insect's back and the youngster wriggles out. Some insects **molt** more than thirty times, but most shed their exoskeleton between four and eight times. Many insects eat their old exoskeletons and reuse the **nutrients** to keep on growing.

When an insect crawls out of its old exoskeleton, it is already enclosed in a new outer coat. While the new covering is soft, moist, and flexible, the insect gulps extra air. This makes its body as large as possible, so that when the new exoskeleton hardens, the insect has some room to grow.

Following a nymph's final molt, it becomes an adult insect with fully formed wings. But a larva must go through an additional growth stage. Following its final molt, a larva becomes a pupa. A pupa doesn't eat a thing, and it usually can't move. During the pupa stage, an insect's body parts are rearranged. As a result, the adult insect that **emerges** looks completely different from the larva.

All adult insects have six legs and three distinct body parts—a head, a **thorax**, and an **abdomen**. The thorax and abdomen are made up of a series of smaller parts called **segments**. These segments make it possible for an insect to bend its body.

Almost all adult insects have wings and can fly. Young insects don't travel very much, but adults need to be more mobile. It is their job to find mates and lay eggs in places where a new **generation** of youngsters can find plenty of food.

What's in a Name?

Most nymphs and larvae have names that help us understand the connection between the youngster and the adult. For example, a monarch caterpillar is the larva of a monarch butterfly. An aphid nymph is the young version of an aphid adult. But sometimes, larva names can be tricky. The larva of a firefly is called a glowworm. Mealworms are young beetles. Cutworms, silkworms, and inchworms are all the larvae of moths.

A Closer Look

Most newly hatched nymphs look like miniature, wingless versions of their parents. Like adults, nymphs have fully developed eyes and **antennae**. They also have the same kind of mouthparts as their parents.

Most nymphs and their adult counterparts have two kinds of eyes. Three small, **simple eyes** on the top of their heads sense light and dark. Two larger, **compound eyes** on either side of their heads are made up of many tiny lenses. A dragonfly may have as many as 28,000 lenses in each compound eye. Each lens sees a small part of the object an insect is looking at. The insect's brain combines all the parts into a single image. Compound eyes help an insect judge distances accurately and notice small movements.

Between the two compound eyes, many nymphs and adults have a pair of antennae. They help the insect feel and smell its surroundings. Some insects also use their antennae to taste and hear.

Most nymphs have the same kind of mouthparts as their parents because they live in the same **habitat** and eat the same kinds of food.

at Nymphs

Dragonfly nymphs and adults have powerful jaws for chewing on insects and other prey. The nymphs and adults of box elder bugs use their piercing mouthparts to suck juices out of plants. All termites have biting mouthparts that help them munch on all kinds of wood.

The major difference between nymphs and adults is their wings. Adults have them, but nymphs don't. When a nymph hatches, it has tiny wing buds. Each time the insect molts, the wing buds become a little bit larger. Following the final molt, a winged adult emerges. After resting for a while so its wings can dry out, the adult zooms into the air.

What Is a Naiad?

While many nymphs live on land, others live in ponds or streams. Some people use the word *naiad* to describe the young water-dwellers. To survive in its watery world, a naiad has gills along its abdomen. During the insect's final molt, its gills are replaced by breathing holes.

9

Dragonflies and Damselflies

Each summer, adult dragonflies and damselflies dart and dip, zoom and zip just above the water's surface. When these hungry hunters aren't patrolling the shoreline for mosquitoes, midges, caddis flies, and other flying insects, they spend most of their time mating. Adult dragonflies and damselflies live only a few weeks, so there's no time to lose.

In midsummer, female green darner dragonflies place their eggs along the stems of water plants. A few weeks later, the nymphs hatch and

A female green darner dragonfly lays eggs while she is still attached to her mate.

This green darner dragonfly nymph is resting at the bottom of a pond.

immediately drop to the bottom of the pond. The dull greenish-brown color of their exoskeletons protects them from hungry **predators** as they wait for a potential meal to pass by.

When a nymph spots a tasty treat, it unfurls the long lower lip folded below its mouth and grabs its **prey**. Then the nymph devours the little animal with its strong jaws. Dragonfly nymphs are not picky

What's the Difference?

Dragonflies and damselflies look very similar and share the same habitat, but there are a few easy ways to tell them apart. An adult damselfly has smaller wings and a thinner body than a dragonfly. When a dragonfly rests, it holds its wings out straight, but a resting damselfly holds its wings above its body. A damselfly nymph has three feathery gills that trail behind its body, but a dragonfly's gills are inside its body.

eaters. They will attack other insects, spiders, worms, slugs, snails, tadpoles, and small fish.

The nymphs eat greedily during summer and autumn, but during the cold winter months, they rest at the bottom of the pond. Most young insects grow up in just a few weeks, but dragonflies may live as nymphs for several years. During that time, they molt between ten and fifteen times.

When it is time for a nymph's final molt, it climbs up a stick or stem until it is out of the water. After a short rest, the dragonfly's outer covering splits open and a soft, damp, pale adult crawls out. As the insect rests next to its old exoskeleton, its crumpled wings dry and expand. About thirty minutes later, the adult dragonfly makes its first flight. Over the next few days, its pale exoskeleton thickens and brilliant colors appear. Soon the insect is an expert flier that can reach speeds of 30 miles (48 kilometers) per hour.

This dragonfly is emerging from its final molt.

Grasshoppers and Crickets

More than 25,000 kinds, or **species**, of grasshoppers and crickets live on Earth. As adults, these insects live in fields and meadows, in trees, or underground. They are known for their ability to leap out of harm's way and for their gentle, buzzing song that fills the summer air.

Each autumn, female eastern lubber grasshoppers dig small holes in the ground, line them with a foamy mixture, and then lay as many as fifty tiny eggs. When the foam dries, it forms a hard **pod** that protects the eggs from hungry predators. After depositing and burying several egg pods, the female grasshoppers die. But all winter long, the nymphs develop in their safe underground homes.

After the first spring rain, each nymph bites through the thin sac surrounding its body and spits out a liquid that softens its eggshell. Using a hard bump on the back of its head, the nymph pushes with all its strength until the egg rips open and it can wriggle out. Then the little insect digs to the surface and sheds the protective covering that surrounds its delicate legs and short antennae.

Like all young insects, eastern lubber grasshopper nymphs spend most of their time feeding. In fact, they eat twice their body weight every day! As the nymphs search for tasty plants, they march across the ground in large groups. Because the group looks like one large creature instead of many tiny insects, most predators leave the nymphs alone.

As the little grasshoppers grow, they molt five times. Following their final molt, they emerge as yellowish-brown adults with black markings. Unlike most full-grown insects, adult lubber grasshoppers have stubby wings that cannot be used for flying. Sharp spikes on their back legs

A group of lubber grasshopper nymphs swarm some plants, spending most of their time eating.

contain a poisonous chemical that sickens any enemies that ignore the grasshoppers' bright warning colors.

Katydids are a group of large green insects with very long antennae. Unlike most of their grasshopper and cricket relatives, true katydids spend nearly all their time in trees or bushes. Most look very similar to leaves, so these insects have no trouble blending into their surroundings. In late summer, male katydids sing for mates by rubbing their wings together.

Because a katydid nymph closely resembles the leaves of the plant that it feeds on, hungry predators have trouble spotting it.

About a week after true katydids mate, the females lay overlapping double rows of flat, oval, gray eggs on bark, leaves, and twigs. The adults die soon after the first frost, but the eggs survive through the long, cold winter and hatch in early spring.

As soon as the ravenous nymphs break out of their eggs, they begin to feed. The young grow quickly and molt every couple of weeks. Each time a nymph outgrows its exoskeleton, it stops eating and remains still. The hard bump on the back of the insect's head swells up with blood and breaks through its hard outer covering. As the nymph wriggles and squirms, the tear spreads down its back. Then the little katydid crawls out. As soon as the new exoskeleton hardens, the insect starts eating again.

After molting five or six times, a full-grown katydid emerges. The new adult swallows a lot of air and pumps extra blood to the surface of its body. This helps the insect's wings unfold as its new outer coat dries and hardens. After about two hours, the katydid is ready for life as an adult.

Lots of Locusts

When very large numbers of young grasshoppers hatch at the same time, the nymphs may develop into adults with unusually short wings. These grasshoppers, called locusts, are very restless and often travel in huge swarms as they search for food.

In the 1870s, people living in the American Midwest reported one swarm of locusts that was 70 miles (112 kilometers) long and 23 miles (37 kilometers) wide. These locusts destroyed millions of dollars worth of crops. They even ate laundry drying on backyard clotheslines.

Mantids and Walkingsticks

Mantids and stick insects are closely related to grasshoppers and crickets. These large insects have long, thin bodies and spend most of their time in grassy fields, bushes, or trees. While mantids are ferocious daytime hunters, stick insects prefer to quietly munch on plants at night.

The most popular member of the mantid family is the praying mantis. This insect's name comes from the way it holds its body as it waits for prey to pass by. Hour after hour, a praying mantis remains perfectly still with its short front legs raised and folded. The bright green insect may look as if it is praying, but it is really trying to blend in with its surroundings.

When a potential meal approaches, the mantid slowly swivels its triangular head and watches the prey with its enormous eyes. As soon as the unsuspecting insect is within range, the praying mantis lunges forward and grasps the prey with its spiny, hooked front legs. Then the hungry hunter devours its catch.

A praying mantis will eat just about anything it can catch, from insects to small snakes and birds. A female praying mantis may even gobble up a male after the insects have mated. The extra energy comes in handy as she searches for a place to lay her eggs. Once the female finds a branch well above the ground, she hangs upside down and squeezes a white, foamy mixture out of her abdomen. When the foamy egg case is about the size of a walnut, she lays 100 to 300 eggs and then looks for a good spot to lay another batch of eggs.

The female dies a few weeks later, but the hard foam case protects her eggs all winter long. In late spring, the nymphs punch through slits on the bottom of the egg case. Then they wriggle free of the thin protective

This praying mantis is about to make a meal of a grasshopper it trapped with its front legs.

Praying mantis nymphs pour out of their egg case in a race to lower themselves to the ground.

sac surrounding their bodies and race to lower themselves to the ground on thin white threads. The nymphs must scurry away before they are eaten by one of their brothers or sisters.

A young praying mantis hunts just like its parents, but it must eat more often to fuel its growth. As a nymph gets bigger and bigger, it must molt between six and nine times. When it is time to shed its exoskeleton, the insect hangs upside down from a twig or stem and waits for its hard outer covering to split in half. Soon after the nymph climbs out of its old exoskeleton, the new one hardens and the insect can return to its never-ending search for prey. Following its final molt, an adult praying mantis flies off in search of a mate.

A walkingstick is a slow-moving, wingless insect that blends perfectly with its surroundings. As long as the walkingstick stays perfectly still, it is nearly impossible to spot among the thin, young branches of a leafy tree.

In the late summer, a female giant walkingstick lays hundreds of tiny eggs. She lets some fall straight to the ground and catapults others by rapidly flicking her abdomen just as she releases an egg. Spreading the eggs over a larger area means that the nymphs won't have to compete for food. Because the eggs look like seeds, they do not attract the attention of most predators.

The eggs may lie on the ground for up to three years, but they always hatch in the spring. To escape from their thick-shelled eggs, the long, thin nymphs push open a special lid at one end. Then the little green insects climb up the nearest plant.

Like their parents, walkingstick nymphs are masters of disguise. During the day they remain still and rest, but if the wind blows, the insects cleverly sway in unison with the plant they are on. At night, the hungry nymphs feed greedily on leaves and stems. As the walkingsticks grow, they molt about once a week. After five or six molts, they emerge as full-grown brownish-gray adults.

Cockroaches and Termites

Cockroaches are among the oldest animals on Earth. Many scientists think that termites **evolved** from cockroaches about 220 million years ago. Both cockroaches and termites are pests. At night, cockroaches scurry around our kitchens in search of crumbs. During the day, termites dine on the wood our homes are made of.

A female German cockroach carries her large egg case at the end of her abdomen. Because she carries the egg case with her until just before the young emerge, German cockroaches are very successful at reproducing.

Cockroaches live just about everywhere and will eat just about anything. The German cockroach is one of the most common species living in North America. About three days after mating, each female lays an egg case containing as many as thirty developing youngsters. For nearly a month, the mother carries her egg case everywhere she goes. Not long after she leaves the case in a dark, safe place, the tiny nymphs break out and begin searching for food.

The hatchlings are soft and white, but they quickly harden and turn dark brown. For the next six months, the nymphs continue to grow and develop. They spend about eighteen hours each day resting, and then feed for a few hours each night. If the nymphs feel threatened, they make a mad dash for a shady corner or squeeze into a tiny crevice.

A growing roach may molt a dozen times. If the little insect accidentally rips off a leg or tears out an antenna as it wriggles out of its old exoskeleton, it's no problem. Within a few days, the lost body part regrows. After the final molt, a full-grown, winged cockroach emerges. Now the insect is ready to begin its life as an adult.

While cockroaches gobble up whatever they can find, termites are a bit more picky. They eat only dead plant material. In warm parts of the world, termites live in giant aboveground nests, but in North America, most termites live in **colonies** in the soil, in woodpiles, or in the foundations of buildings.

Each spring, a few males and females leave their nest, find mates, and start a new colony. When the nymphs hatch, they are completely helpless. Their parents, the king and queen, feed the youngsters **regurgitated** food until they are full grown. But the new adults do not leave to start another colony. They become workers that care for the next batch of eggs.

As the eastern **subterranean** termite colony grows, the nymphs develop different kinds of bodies and become members of different **castes**. Each termite caste plays a special role in the colony. Most nymphs become workers that collect food and take care of the eggs and nymphs. Some youngsters develop long, armored heads and large jaws during

If you look closely, you can see a variety of castes in this termite colony. The nymphs are small and pale, the workers are large and dark, and the soldiers have large orange heads. There are no swarmers here.

Compared to the soldier termites around her, the queen is huge.

their final molt. These soldiers defend the colony against ants and other predators. Swarmers are the only termites that can mate and produce young. As these nymphs grow and molt they develop long black bodies and wings, so they can travel far from the nest.

After three or four years, a termite colony may include more than 60,000 workers, and the queen may lay thousands of eggs each day. A queen termite can live many years and grow to be more than 5 inches (13 centimeters) long. When she dies, a female swarmer usually takes her place.

That's Incredible!

Cockroaches can run faster than any other insect in the world. If a cockroach were the size of a person, it would be able to travel 225 miles (360 kilometers) per hour. No human can run anywhere near that fast!

Why Stinkbugs Stink

Have you ever eaten a piece of fruit that tasted bad but didn't look rotten? That nasty taste was probably stinkbug juice. Wherever stinkbugs go, they leave behind sticky, smelly goo. Young or old, all stinkbugs smell bad and taste worse. It's their way of persuading enemies to leave them alone.

True Bugs

Some people use the word *bug* to describe all small, flying, or crawling critters, but bugs are really just one group of insects. More than 40,000 species of true bugs live on Earth. Most have wings that cross over their shield-shaped backs. If you see an insect with an "X" pattern on its back, it's probably a true bug. Some common true bugs include stinkbugs, bedbugs, giant water bugs, water striders, and box elder bugs.

After spending the winter in a sheltered place, female box elder bugs fly off in search of a quick meal of tasty leaves. While these insects prefer box elder trees, they also live and feed on other kinds of maple trees and fruit trees.

With their energy restored, the females lay dozens of eggs along the tree's bark and leaves. A couple of weeks later the eggs hatch and hundreds of tiny nymphs burst into the world. All summer long the little bugs eat and grow. They spend most of their time feeding alongside the adults. All box elder bugs use their sucking mouthparts to slurp the juices out of leaves, buds, and young twigs.

After five molts, the nymphs emerge as adults. But their life doesn't change much until late summer. Then the adults pair up and mate. A few

These box elder bug nymphs look similar to the adult among them. The adult is a bit larger and darker in color, and it has wings.

weeks later the males die, but the females survive until spring, when they lay a new generation of eggs.

A giant water bug has a very different kind of life. The two tiny breathing tubes on the tip of its abdomen make it possible for this insect

This male giant water bug is carrying eggs on its back. Most nymphs have already hatched, but three of them are still close by.

to spend most of its life underwater. And while box elder bugs quietly sip plant juices, giant water bugs spend their days hunting insects, tadpoles, small fish, and salamanders.

After two giant water bugs mate, the female wraps her legs around the male, spreads glue all over his back, and lays more than one hundred eggs there. The eggs will be safe from most predators while the little nymphs develop inside.

By early summer the youngsters are ready to hatch. Using a set of special spines called an "egg burster," each nymph breaks out of its egg and swims to the surface for its first breath of fresh air. Over the next few weeks, most of the hungry hatchlings eat one another. The survivors grow quickly and are soon ready for larger prey.

When a young giant water bug spots a potential meal, it grabs the prey with its large folding front legs. The victim has little chance of

A giant water bug feeds on a small fish with its piercing mouthpart.

escaping from the nymph's tight grip. Next, the water bug pierces the prey with its strong, sharp beak and sucks out all the body juices.

Because giant water bug nymphs can catch large prey, they grow quickly and shed their exoskeletons about once a week. After five molts, adult giant water bugs emerge and continue life in their watery world.

Cicadas and Aphids

Cicadas and aphids belong to a large group of insects that is closely related to the true bugs. Like grasshoppers and crickets, male cicadas "sing" for their mates. On hot summer days, these insects buzz loudly by vibrating special muscles in their abdomens.

After mating, female seventeen-year cicadas slit open the bark of tree branches and lay rows of eggs inside. When the nymphs hatch, they drop to the ground and dig into the soil. For the next seventeen years, the nymphs live underground. As they sip sap from plant roots, the youngsters slowly grow and molt, grow and molt.

Just before their final molt, the nymphs dig to the surface and climb up the nearest tree or telephone pole. After a short rest, the insect's exoskeleton breaks open and splits down its back. The adult cicada struggles out, leaving behind the empty exoskeleton. At first, the cicada is soft and white, but its new covering stiffens and darkens quickly. As soon as its wings dry out, the insect flies off in search of a mate.

Cicadas take a long time to grow up, but the steps of their life cycle are similar to those of most other insects that go through simple metamorphosis. Aphids may pass through three life stages, but their life cycle is far from simple.

In late summer, adult rose aphids mate, and the females lay eggs on the stems of rose plants. As the air temperature drops, the adults die, but the hardy eggs survive until spring. As soon as the nymphs hatch, they begin to feed. Using their sucking mouthparts, the little aphids slurp plant juices all day long. The nymphs grow quickly and after several molts they emerge as wingless female adults.

During its final molt, an adult cicada emerges soft and white from its exoskeleton.

How many generations of aphids can you find on this rose stem?

Without mating, these females give birth to a new generation of young. The new nymphs don't hatch out of eggs. They develop inside their mother's body and are born fully developed, like human babies. Like their mothers, these nymphs develop into wingless females that give birth to still more wingless nymphs. By mid-summer, a huge colony of aphids lives on the rose plant.

When the colony becomes over-crowded, a generation of winged adults is born. These females fly to another plant and, without mating, give birth to even more wingless nymphs. In late summer, a second group of winged adult females is born. These aphids fly back to the rose plant and finally give birth to a genera-tion of aphids with both males and females. After these wingless adults mate, the females lay eggs that will hatch the following spring.

Did You Know?

As many as ten generations of aphids may be born in a single summer. And all those aphids need food to live and grow. Even though aphids have many enemies, they do more damage to farmers' crops than any other kind of insect.

A Closer Look

While most nymphs look similar to the adults they will become, most larvae look completely different from their parents. They have no wings, no compound eyes, and no antennae. In fact, most larvae look more like a worm than an adult insect.

Because larvae look so different from adults, many have special names. The crawling larvae of butterflies and moths are called **caterpillars**. The pale, sluggish larvae of many beetles and bees are called **grubs**. The wriggling, legless larvae of most flies are called **maggots**.

Most larvae look and behave differently from their adult counterparts because they live in a different habitat and eat different kinds of foods. As a result, adults and larvae don't compete with one another. While viceroy caterpillars spend their days munching on leaves, viceroy butterflies get all their energy by sipping sugary **nectar**. Similarly, mosquito larvae, called wrigglers, dine on **bacteria**, while adults feed on plant juices and blood.

at Larvae

As a larva molts, its color may change several times. But its shape stays the same. The insect's shape doesn't change until it goes through its pupal stage. During this stage, the insect's body seems stiff and rigid on the outside, but there's a lot going on just below the surface. The insect's larval organs are broken apart, rearranged, and used to build adult body structures. In just a few days, weeks, or months, a fully developed adult forms. Soon after the adult insect emerges, its exoskeleton hardens and its wings expand. Then it takes off in search of a mate.

An Insect World

Three out of every four animals in the world are insects. Scientists estimate that more than one million species of insects live on Earth. More than 80 percent of all known insect species go through complete metamorphosis.

Flies and Mosquitoes

Even though adult flies and mosquitoes have just one pair of wings, they are the best insect fliers in the world. They can zip along, spin, hover, and even fly backward. What's the secret of their success? They have special club-shaped structures called **halteres** that help them keep their balance and fine-tune their flight path.

Mosquitoes are small, fragile insects best known for sucking blood and carrying dangerous diseases. But most of the time, mosquitoes feed on flower nectar. In fact, males never dine on blood, and females only seek out a blood meal a few hours before laying their eggs. Without the proteins in blood, mosquito larvae will not develop properly.

In spring and early summer, female common mosquitoes stack hundreds of eggs to form small, floating rafts on the surface of puddles, natural pools, and ponds. A few days later, each little larva hatches through a special trapdoor at the bottom of its egg. Then it wriggles to the bottom of the pond and begins feeding on bacteria. When the wriggler has had its fill, it returns to the surface and hangs head-down, so it can breathe through a tiny tube in its tail.

Over the next three weeks, the wriggler grows quickly and molts four times. During this time, it changes from a ravenous, colorless hatchling to a creamy-white, comma-shaped pupa that floats on the surface of the water and doesn't eat a thing. Less than a week later, the pupa's outer covering splits open, and a winged adult darts into the sky.

Although young mosquitoes are called wrigglers, the larvae of most flies are called maggots. A housefly maggot enters the world just a few hours after its mother has laid her eggs. Along with its one hundred

These mosquito larvae are hanging upside down in water so they can breathe through their tails. A small white pupa, which will soon turn into an adult, is floating at the surface.

Medical Maggots

Long ago, doctors discovered that blowfly maggots could be used to clean out deep wounds. Because the larvae devoured harmful bacteria and injured tissue, wounds were less likely to become infected. Eventually, better treatments were discovered, but even the new techniques don't always do their job. That's why a few modern doctors have started experimenting with maggots. When standard treatments fail to cure bedsores or **gangrene**, the doctors add maggots to their patients' wounds. In many cases, the patients have improved.

brothers and sisters, the little larva eats its egg and then starts to feed on anything else it can find. Most females lay their oval white eggs in moist, warm manure, among garbage, or inside the carcass of a dead animal. All these habitats can provide the small, wormlike maggots with plenty of food.

By the time the housefly larvae are a day old, they have doubled in size and must shed their exoskeletons. During the next few days, the maggots continue to eat and grow and molt. After their third molt, the larvae look for a cool place to hide. As the insects rest, their exoskeletons turn yellow and then reddish brown. Now they are pupae.

Each pupa remains quiet and still. But inside, the insect is changing rapidly. The wormlike body is developing a head with compound eyes and antennae. Wings and long, slender legs are growing out of the thorax.

A few days later one end of the pupal case bursts open, and the head of an adult fly pops out. Using a hard notch on the top of its head, the fly tears the case open

Small white maggots turn into the reddish-brown pupae. These pupae will become darker just before the adults emerge.

This housefly is emerging from its pupal case.

and wriggles out. After the fly has a short rest, its wings are dry, and it is ready to begin life as an adult. Most adult houseflies live for only about three weeks, so they must work quickly to find a mate and lay a new generation of eggs.

Beetles

One third of all the insects alive today are beetles. With more than 300,000 species, beetles come in many different sizes, shapes, and colors. The most popular beetle in North America is the ladybug.

In early spring, two-spotted ladybug females attach clusters of bright yellow eggs to the leaves and stems of plants. After a few days the eggs turn white, and a dozen pale larvae force their way into the world. Within a few hours, their little bodies turn black. By that time the ladybug larvae have started hunting their favorite foods—aphids and scale insects. Some larvae eat as many as fifty aphids a day!

The more the larvae eat, the faster they grow. Because an insect's exoskeleton cannot stretch as it grows, a ladybug larva must molt four times. After the second molt, the larva has an orange pattern on its body.

About a month after the larva hatches, it stops feeding, attaches itself to a leaf or stem, and molts for the last time. Now the ladybug is a pupa. The insect's new orange covering takes a few hours to harden. During this time, a black pattern appears on the pupal case.

For about five days the pupa doesn't move. But an incredible transformation is going on inside the hard case. The ladybug's body is becoming shorter and rounder. The insect is also developing wings, compound eyes, and antennae.

When the adult beetle is ready to emerge, it stretches its body until the pupal case cracks and splits open at one end. The ladybug pokes out its head and then pulls out the rest of its pale orange body. As the ladybug's body darkens, spots appear on its back. At the same time, the

These two-spotted ladybug larvae are shedding their exoskeletons.

insect's wings slowly dry out. After a few hours the full-grown beetle is ready to begin life as an adult.

Young ladybugs are usually called larvae, but most people use the word *grub* to describe other kinds of beetle larvae. The pale, wormlike grubs of green June beetles hatch out of round gray eggs laid in the soil.

A June beetle grub's body is so fat that it can hardly move. If a predator spots this grub, the little insect will curl up and play dead.

Most beetles live on land, but some spend most of their time in the water. The larvae of predaceous diving beetles are called "water tigers" because they are such ferocious predators. Water tigers live underwater and breathe through gills. As adults, these insects have lungs and breathe air. Each time the adult beetles dive below the surface, they must store a bubble of air under each wing and take a few gulps whenever they need it.

All summer long the grubs rest during the day. At night they munch on plant roots. As the youngsters feed, they slowly wriggle and crawl through the soil.

As winter approaches, the grubs stop eating, **burrow** farther underground, and rest until warm weather returns. In spring the grubs move closer to the surface. Each one finds a sheltered spot and molts for the last time. Now it is a pupa enclosed in a tough golden case.

For about a month the beetle pupa remains quiet and still while the insect transforms its body. In June or July, the hard case cracks open, and the adult carefully pushes and pulls until it is free. Within a few hours, the adult green June beetle's pale exoskeleton hardens and darkens. The insect rests until dusk and then flies off in search of sugary nectar and fruit. Then it is time to find a mate and start a family of its own.

June beetle pupae look very different from grubs. Inside the pupal case, the insects' bodies transform into adults.

Bees, Wasps, and Ants

Like termites, many bees, wasps, and ants are social insects. They live in large colonies, and each insect has a special job. As many as 60,000 adult insects may live in a honeybee hive. Most of these bees are female workers. They gather pollen and nectar, feed the larvae, keep the hive clean, build and repair the hive's six-sided honeycombs, and defend the hive from enemies. About one hundred male drones live in the hive. Their only job is to mate with the queen.

From February to November, the queen lays one thousand to two thousand eggs each day. She deposits each one at the bottom of a cell in the honeycomb. After about three days the shells of the eggs dissolve, and wormlike grubs appear. The helpless larvae remain in their honeycomb cells and are fed by adult workers.

At first, the workers feed the grubs a sweet syrup called royal jelly. The youngsters eat so much that their weight increases more than five

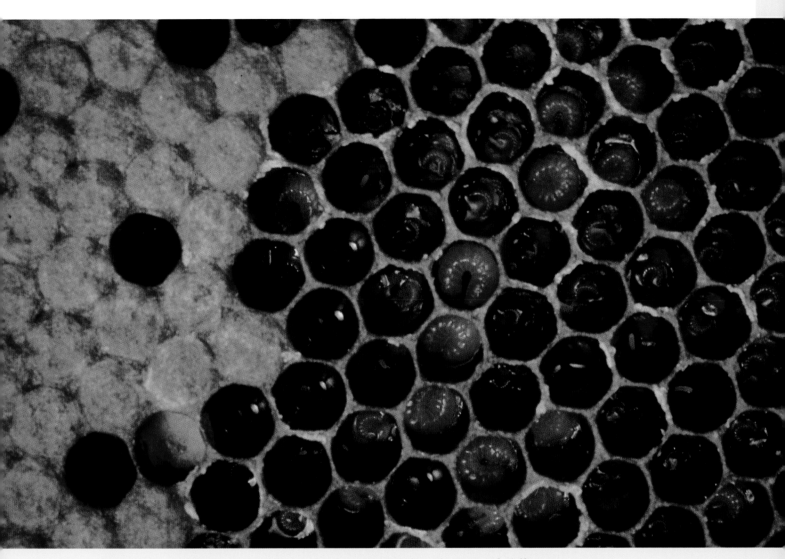

The open cells of this honeycomb show honeybee larvae of different sizes—some fill the entire cell while others are barely visible. The closed cells (left) house pupae that are in the midst of transforming into adults.

times in just one day. After three days, the larvae that will become workers or drones start to eat beebread—a mixture of honey and pollen. The little bees grow so quickly that they must molt every single day.

When the grubs are five days old, they molt for the last time and spin a **cocoon** around themselves. Now they are pupae. Workers cover each pupa's cell with wax, so the insect will not be bothered while it transforms itself. About a week later, each new adult chews its way out of its cell. Most adult honeybees live only a few weeks, but a queen may live as long as four years.

Like honeybees, paper wasps and yellow jackets live in nests and work together to raise their young. But some wasps have a very different way of making sure their larvae will have plenty of food. In spring, female braconid wasps use long, needlelike structures to lay eggs inside the bodies of caterpillars or beetle grubs. When the wasp larvae hatch, they begin to feed on their **host**'s body fat. As the larvae continue to grow, they eat more and more of their host's insides.

After the final molt, each little wasp tunnels through its host's tough exoskeleton and builds a white oval cocoon on top of its back. By this time, the host's body may be nothing but an empty shell. About a week later the top of the pupa's cocoon pops open, and an adult wasp zips into the air.

While most adult insects have wings and can fly, most ants are wingless. In early spring, a few winged males and females meet in the air and mate. A few days later, the males die, and the females lose their wings. But by this time, each queen has returned to the anthill where she grew up.

The little black ant queen starts laying eggs right away. About two weeks later the first eggs hatch, and pale, wormlike larvae appear. As

This caterpillar is host to braconid wasp larvae and many small white wasp cocoons. A few newly emerged adults are also seen here.

These little black worker ants take care of the pupae until they turn into adults.

female worker ants return to the anthill, they regurgitate food and feed it to the hungry larvae. The youngsters grow quickly. During the next three weeks, they molt four or five times.

Following their final molt, the young ants spin cocoons and become pupae. The workers watch the pupae carefully. If they get too hot or too cold, the workers move them to another area of the nest. After two or three weeks, the ants' larval body parts have been completely rearranged. When the insects are ready, they break out of their cocoons and start life as adult ants.

Moths and Butterflies

Caterpillars, the larvae of butterflies and moths, are the most familiar young insects. You've probably seen an inchworm munching on leaves or a banded woolly bear crawling across the ground. But because caterpillars look so different from the adult insects they will become, you may not know that both inchworms and banded woolly bears transform into moths that cruise the night skies.

Woolly bear caterpillars are actually the larvae of moths.

The most popular butterfly in North America is the monarch. In spring and summer the brightly colored females lay eggs on the undersides of milkweed leaves. Three days later each caterpillar chews a hole in its egg and wriggles out. Then it spins a silky thread that will act like a safety line as the caterpillar crawls along the bottom of the leaf. Now that it is safe, the little larva devours the rest of its egg. Then it starts munching on milkweed leaves.

As a monarch caterpillar grows, its rigid exoskeleton becomes tighter and tighter. Finally, the larva stops eating. It twists, squirms, and wriggles until its outer covering breaks open and then cracks all the way down its back. When the larva emerges from its old exoskeleton, its new coat is still soft. The caterpillar fills its body with air to stretch the flexible

A large and a small monarch caterpillar on a milkweed plant

covering as much as possible. The insect rests until the exoskeleton hardens, and then it starts to eat again.

During the next two weeks, the caterpillar continues to grow quickly. It must molt three more times. Just before its final molt, the monarch caterpillar attaches itself to a branch or twig with a bit of silk. As the monarch sheds its old coat it becomes a pupa. The hard shell that surrounds the pupa is called a **chrysalis**.

On the left, a monarch caterpillar is becoming a pupa. On the right, a protective chrysalis is already surrounding a pupa.

A beautiful adult monarch butterfly begins to emerge from its chrysalis.

Over the next two weeks, something incredible happens. The fat, clumsy caterpillar transforms into a beautiful butterfly. When the chrysalis splits open, the adult insect begins to emerge. First, it pushes its legs and antennae through the opening. Once it has a firm hold on the outside of the chrysalis, the butterfly pulls the rest of its body out of the case and rests.

At first, the insect's body is wet and sticky. As it dries, the butterfly stretches its crumpled wings. After about thirty minutes the monarch is ready for its first flight. It takes off in search of its first sugar meal of nectar.

Adult monarchs fly south for the winter and mate in early spring, but most adult moths and butterflies have much shorter lives. Female luna moths lay their dark, round eggs on the leaves of birch, hickory, or walnut trees. About ten days later, the caterpillars munch through the shells of their eggs and crawl out. For the next five or six weeks, they eat and grow, eat and grow. A larva's bright colors make it easy to spot, but sharp spines along its back help protect it from enemies.

A luna moth caterpillar munches on the leaf of a sweet-gum tree.

A newly hatched female luna moth rests while her crumpled wings dry off and begin to expand.

Each time the caterpillars outgrow their hard coat, they shed their exoskeletons. After four molts the full-grown luna larvae crawl to the ground. Each one wraps itself in a leaf and weaves it closed with silk. All winter long the pupa stays safe inside its cocoon. While the wind blows and the snow falls, the insect's body is changing.

On a late spring morning the luna is ready for life as an adult. It tears open its cocoon and wriggles out. The insect slowly crawls up a nearby plant and rests while a gentle breeze dries its wings. By dusk the luna moth's wings have expanded, and it is ready to fly. As the insect glides through the moonlit sky it looks for a mate.

Glossary

abdomen—the back section of an insect's body

antennae—body structures that insects use to sense movements and understand their surroundings

bacterium (pl. bacteria)—a tiny, one-celled organism that is neither a plant nor an animal

caterpillar—the second stage in the life of a moth or butterfly

chrysalis—the case or covering in which a butterfly transforms from a larva to an adult

cocoon—the case or covering in which moths and some other insect species transform from larvae to adults

compound eye—one of two large eyes on the sides of an insect's head

emerge—to come out

exoskeleton—the hard, protective outer layer that covers the bodies of insects, spiders, and other animals that do not have a backbone

gangrene—a medical condition in which body parts begin to decay because blood vessels cannot carry oxygen and nutrients to cells

generation—a group of organisms that hatch or are born at the same time

grub—the second stage in the life of most beetles and bees

habitat—the place where a plant or animal lives

haltere—one of the club-shaped structures that helps a fly keep its balance and steer as it flies through the air

host—a living plant or animal that provides another creature with food or a place to live

larva (pl. larvae)—the second stage in the life of amphibians and many invertebrates, including insects that go through complete metamorphosis

maggot—the second stage in the life of most flies

metamorphosis—the process by which insects and other invertebrates become adults

molt—to shed an old exoskeleton that is too small

nectar—a sugary liquid that many flowers produce; it attracts insect pollinators

nutrient—a substance, especially in food, that is needed for healthy growth

pod—a dry case that contains grasshopper eggs

predator—an animal that hunts and kills other animals for food

prey—an animal that is hunted, killed, and eaten by another animal

pupa (pl. pupae)—the third stage in the life of insects that go through complete metamorphosis

regurgitate—to spit up partially digested food

segment—one of the small sections of an insect's body. Because an insect has segments, it can bend its hard exoskeleton.

simple eyes—a set of eyes that insects use to sense light and dark

species—a group of organisms that share certain characteristics and can mate and produce healthy young

subterranean—underground

thorax—the middle section of an insect's body, where the legs are attached

To Find Out More

Books

Goor, Ron, and Nancy Goor. *Insect Metamorphosis: From Egg to Adult*. New York: Atheneum, 1990.

Kite, Patricia L. *Insect Facts and Folklore*. Brookfield, CT: The Millbrook Press, 2001.

Markle, Sandra. *Creepy, Crawly Baby Bugs*. New York: Walker & Company, 1996.

Pipe, Jim, and Mike Taylor. *The Giant Book of Bugs and Creepy Crawlies*. Brookfield, CT: The Millbrook Press, 1998.

Silverstein, Alvin, Virginia Silverstein, and Laura Silverstein Nunn. *Creepy Crawlies*. Brookfield, CT: The Millbrook Press, 2003.

Stewart, Melissa. *Insects*. Danbury, CT: Children's Press, 2001.

Wilsdon, Christina. *National Audubon Society First Guide to Insects*. New York: Scholastic, 1997.

Web Sites

Maggot Study
http://gateway.drew.buffalo.k12.ny.us/drew/kidprojects/museum/
MaggotSShtml/Slide1.html
This site describes how a group of sixth graders in Buffalo, New York, collected and studied maggots they discovered in a tree hole.

The University of Florida Book of Insect Records
http://ufbir.ifas.ufl.edu/
Have you ever wondered which insect flies the fastest or has the longest life cycle? You'll find the answers to these questions and many other fascinating insect facts at this site.

The Wonderful World of Insects
http://www.earthlife.net/insects/six.html
Have you ever found an insect, but weren't sure exactly what kind of insect it was? This site can help you identify all kinds of creepy crawlers. You can also learn how different groups of insects are related to one another, and ask experts questions about insects.

Index

Page numbers in *italics* refer to illustrations.

About the Author

Melissa Stewart earned a bachelor's degree in biology from Union College and a master's degree in science and environmental journalism from New York University. She has written more than thirty books for children and contributed articles to a variety of magazines for adults and children. Her work has appeared in *Natural New England*, *Science World*, *Odyssey*, *ChemMatters*, *National Geographic World*, *Wild Outdoor World*, and *American Heritage of Invention and Technology*. Ms. Stewart lives in Marlborough, Massachusetts. In her free time, she enjoys reading, canoeing, and exploring natural areas in search of insects and other wildlife.